D0771167

# Stadiums

## By Virginia Loh-Hagan

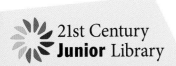
21st Century
**Junior** Library

Published in the United States of America by
**Cherry Lake Publishing**
Ann Arbor, Michigan
www.cherrylakepublishing.com

Content Adviser: Dr. Todd Kelley, Associate Professor of Engineering/Technology Teacher Education, Purdue Polytechnic Institute, West Lafayette, Indiana
Reading Adviser: Marla Conn MS, Ed., Literacy specialist, Read-Ability, Inc.

Photo Credits: © badahos/Shutterstock Images, cover; © Joyce Vincent/Shutterstock Images, 4; © Stacia_S/Shutterstock Images, 6; © Worakit Sirijinda/Shutterstock Images, 8; © Igor Iakovlev/Shutterstock Images, 10; © Joy Brown/Shutterstock Images, 12; © Jurand/Shutterstock Images, 14; © Susan Montgomery/Shutterstock Images, 16; © Neil Wigmore/Shutterstock Images, 18

Library of Congress Cataloging-in-Publication Data
Names: Loh-Hagan, Virginia, author.
Title: Stadiums / by Virginia Loh-Hagan.
Description: Ann Arbor : Cherry Lake Publishing, [2017] | Series: Extraordinary Engineering | Includes bibliographical references
   and index. | Audience: Grades: K to Grade 3.
Identifiers: LCCN 2016032398| ISBN 9781634721660 (hardcover) | ISBN 9781634722322 (pdf) | ISBN 9781634722988
   (paperback) | ISBN 9781634723640 (ebook)
Subjects: LCSH: Stadiums—Juvenile literature. | Stadiums—Design and construction—Juvenile literature.
Classification: LCC GV415 .L64 2017 | DDC 796.06/8—dc23
LC record available at https://lccn.loc.gov/2016032398

Cherry Lake Publishing would like to acknowledge the work of The Partnership for 21st Century Learning.
Please visit *www.p21.org* for more information.

Printed in the United States of America
Corporate Graphics

# CONTENTS

The Rogers Centre is a stadium in Toronto, Canada, that has hosted baseball, basketball, soccer, and football games.

# What Are Stadiums?

Stadiums host big events. Some have stages. Most have fields. Stadiums seat many **spectators**. Spectators are watchers. They watch sports games. They watch music shows. Most stadiums are **open air**. Some are covered. Some stadiums host baseball games. They're called **ballparks**. Stadiums are not **arenas**. Arenas host smaller indoor events, like basketball and hockey games.

The Colosseum is in Rome. It's a famous ancient stadium.

Stadiums have fields in the middle. Seats surround the field. There are three basic stadium designs. Oval-shaped stadiums have seats all the way around. They're large. **Horseshoe** stadiums are open at one end. They are U-shaped. Open stadiums are open at both ends.

# Look!

Look at pictures of a stadium. Or go visit your local stadium. What type is it? How many seats does it have? What is it used for?

Stadiums must have strong **foundations**.

# How Do Stadiums Resist Forces?

Stadiums are **anchored** in the ground. Solid rock holds them in place. **Load** travels down to the ground. This spreads out weight. Stadiums have steel **superstructures**. They have thin steel rods. Rods are wrapped in **concrete**. They're like steel tubes. This makes stadiums strong. Rods hold the concrete together.

Braces are added to superstructures.

Stadiums resist **forces**. Forces include wind and earthquakes. Engineers use **braces** to design stadiums. Braces bend. They don't snap easily. They take in forces. They spread out forces.

Football stadiums are designed to run north to south. This way, sunlight won't bother players. Baseball stadiums let wind whip through them. Wind travels up over the top. It speeds down to the field. Then, it goes over the other side. Wind can affect how balls fly.

Top seats are called "nosebleed" seats.

# How Do Stadiums Help Spectators See?

Large stadiums can seat over 100,000 people. They have fold-down seats. This saves space. This lets people sit or stand. Seats are set in rows. Rows are at different levels. Seats start at field level. They rise to the top. Top rows are higher in the sky. This **tiered** seating lets people have clear views. People can see from all angles.

These special beams are called cantilevers.

Older stadiums used poles. These poles provided support. But they blocked people's views. Engineers solved this problem. They started using special beams. The beams are only supported at one end. They move load to the supported end. So, engineers don't need to place posts between people and the field. This ensures people have clear views.

# Ask Questions!

Ask friends or family if they've been to a stadium. Which one? What were they doing there? Did they like their seats?

The University of Michigan Big House holds 109,901 noisy fans.

# How Do Stadiums Handle Sound?

Fans make a lot of noise. They cheer for their teams. They stomp their feet. They dance. Their sounds travel down to the players. Players play better.

Stadiums are shaped like bowls. They trap sounds. They make sounds louder. Engineers try to design stadium bowls to be as small as possible. They want to keep in sounds.

Curves and angles affect how sound travels.

Sound loses energy as it travels. Sound travels in waves. It **vibrates**. It puts pressure in the air. Engineers build reflecting surfaces. They use wood, concrete, and metal. This bounces sounds back to the crowds. Some stadiums have roofs. Roofs can **amp** up noise. Sound travels up. Roofs bounce sound back down.

# Think!

Think about why cities want stadiums. Think about why cities don't want stadiums. Read about the pros and cons of stadiums.

# Try This!

## Materials

4 feet (1.2m) of yarn, 2 spoons
of different sizes, wooden ruler

## Procedures

1 Make a loop in the middle of
  the yarn. Tie it around handle of smaller spoon.

2 Pull tightly. Have spoon hang in the center of the yarn. Two
  pieces of yarn will hang on each side.

3 Take one end of yarn. Wrap around pointer finger. Do
  this for each hand.

4 Place tip of fingers into ears. Hold.

5 Have spoon hang below waist.

6 Get a friend to help. Have the friend hold the ruler. Have
  friend gently hit the spoon's round part.

7 Listen. Small spoons make a bell sound. Try this with the larger spoon. Large spoons make a gong sound. (Everyone else hears a tinkling. This is the sound of the ruler hitting the spoon.)

## Principle at Play

This activity shows how sound waves work. The ruler hits the spoon. This creates sound waves. These waves travel up the yarn. They travel to the ears. They don't spread out in space. The yarn is a conductor. Conductors allow sound waves to travel. Use different spoon sizes. Change size of yarn. Change type of yarn. Use forks. Listen for different sounds. Think about what affects sound waves.

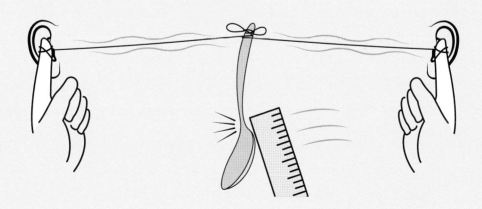

# GLOSSARY

**amp** (AMP) to make louder

**anchored** (ANG-kurd) firmly placed in the ground

**arenas** (uh-REE-nuhz) public buildings that host indoor events

**ballparks** (BAWL-pahrks) stadiums designed to host baseball games

**braces** (BRASE-iz) devices that clamp things tightly together or give support

**concrete** (KAHN-kreet) building material made from a mixture of sand, gravel, cement, and water that becomes very hard when it dries

**forces** (FORS-iz) pushing or pulling motions

**foundations** (foun-DAY-shuhnz) the stable structure on which a building is constructed

**horseshoe** (HORS-shoo) having a U-shape

**load** (LOHD) where weight falls in a building

**open air** (OH-puhn AIR) having no roof, out in the open

**spectators** (SPEK-tay-turz) watchers

**superstructures** (SOO-pur-struhk-churz) frameworks

**tiered** (TEERD) leveled, stepped

**vibrates** (VYE-brates) moves rapidly to and fro

# FIND OUT MORE

## BOOKS

Hurley, Michael. *The World's Most Amazing Stadiums*. Chicago: Raintree, 2012.

Mooney, Carla. *Stadiums and Coliseums*. Vero Beach, FL: Rourke Educational Media, 2015.

Mullins, Matt. *How Did They Build That? Stadium*. Ann Arbor, MI: Cherry Lake Publishing, 2010.

## WEB SITES

**How Stuff Works—How Do Retractable Roofs in Convertible Stadiums Work?**
http://entertainment.howstuffworks.com/question591.htm
This article provides information about retractable stadium roofs.

**National Geographic Kids—Ten Facts About the Colosseum!**
www.ngkids.co.uk/history/colosseum
This site presents facts about ancient Rome's Colosseum, which inspired today's stadiums.

# INDEX

# ABOUT THE AUTHOR

Dr. Virginia Loh-Hagan is an author, university professor, former classroom teacher, and curriculum designer. She likes tailgating in stadium parking lots. She lives in San Diego with her very tall husband and very naughty dogs. To learn more about her, visit www.virginialoh.com.